DISCARD

EXPLORING DINOSAURS

STEGOSAURUS

By Susan H. Gray

THE CHILD'S WORLD
CHANHASSEN, MINNESOTA

Published in the United States of America by The Child's World®
P.O. Box 326, Chanhassen, MN 55317-0326
800-599-READ
www.childsworld.com

Content Adviser:
Peter Makovicky,
Ph.D., Curator,
Field Museum,
Chicago, Illinois

Photo Credits: Ben Klaffke: 6, 25; Bettmann/Corbis: 7, 18; ML Sinibaldi/Corbis: 19; Dave G. Houser/Corbis: 24; CRD Photo/Corbis: 26; Richard Cummins/Corbis: 27; Francois Gohier/Photo Researchers, Inc.: 5; Ludek Pesek/Science Photo Library/Photo Researchers, Inc.: 9, 21; Salisbury District Hospital/Science Photo Library/Photo Researchers, Inc.: 10–11; Science, Industry & Business Library/New York Public Library/Science Photo Library/Photo Researchers, Inc.: 14; Joe Tucciarone/Science Photo Library/Photo Researchers, Inc.: 22, 23; Michael Brett-Surman/Courtesy of the Smithsonian Institution: 12; Ken Lucas/Visuals Unlimited, Inc.: 8, 15; C.P. George/Visuals Unlimited, Inc.: 13; A.J. Copley/Visuals Unlimited, Inc.: 17.

The Child's World®: Mary Berendes, Publishing Director

Editorial Directions, Inc.: E. Russell Primm, Editorial Director; Dana Meachen Rau, Line Editor; Katie Marsico, Assistant Editor; Matthew Messbarger, Editorial Assistant; Susan Hindman, Copy Editor; Susan Ashley, Proofreader; Tim Griffin, Indexer; Kerry Reid, Fact Checker; Dawn Friedman, Photo Reseacher; Linda S. Koutris, Photo Selector

Original cover art by Todd Marshall

The Design Lab: Kathleen Petelinsek, Design and Page Production

Library of Congress Cataloging-in-Publication Data
Gray, Susan Heinrichs.
  Stegosaurus / by Susan H. Gray.
      p. cm.— (Exploring dinosaurs)
Includes index.
Summary: Describes what is known about the physical characteristics, behavior, habitat, and life cycle of this slow-moving vegetarian dinosaur.
  ISBN 1-59296-044-8 (lib. bdg. : alk. paper)
  1. Stegosaurus—Juvenile literature. [1. Stegosaurus. 2. Dinosaurs.] I. Title. II. Series.
QE862.O65G7458 2004
567.915'3—dc22   2003018631

TABLE OF CONTENTS

CHAPTER ONE

SPIKE

It was a warm day, and a gentle rain was falling. The dinosaur had spent most of her morning munching on ferns. But now she stopped eating, walked a little ways, then lay down. The rain made a soft pattering sound on her thick skin. Today, she just didn't feel well. One of her tail spikes had a bad **infection,** and it wasn't getting any better. The infection had spread throughout her whole body. Now it was making her sick. She closed her heavy eyelids and took one last, deep breath.

One hundred and fifty million years later, scientists in Colorado found her skeleton. It was embedded in rock. It was broken in places and needed lots of cleaning. And the scientists noticed that one of her tail spikes was different from the others. They were excited to

This Stegosaurus *skeleton at the Royal Tyrrell Museum in Canada is similar to the one discovered by scientists in Colorado. Scientists believe Spike may have become sick from the infection in one of her tail spikes after the spike was somehow broken.*

make such a find. The scientists worked on the skeleton for months

and months. They decided it belonged to a *Stegosaurus* (STEG-oh-

SORE-uhss) and it was probably a female. They named her Spike.

CHAPTER TWO

WHAT IS A STEGOSAURUS?

A *Stegosaurus* is a dinosaur that lived about 150 million to 144 million years ago. Its name is taken from Greek words that mean "covered lizard" or "roofed lizard." The name refers to two rows of bony plates that ran along the dinosaur's back. Seventeen triangular plates ran from the dinosaur's neck down to its tail. Around its throat,

Two pairs of spikes on the tail of this Stegosaurus *skeleton were once powerful weapons. Unfortunately, although these spikes were often used for protection, they also slowed the animal down. While* Stegosaurus *could fight with its spiky tail, the dinosaur would have found it difficult to outrun enemies.*

Stegosaurus had a protective bib of bony plates. At the very end of its tail, it had pairs of huge spikes about 3 feet (1 meter) long.

Stegosaurus was an enormous **reptile.** It stood about 9 feet (2.75 m) tall. It reached a length of up to 30 feet (9 m). It was about as long and tall as a

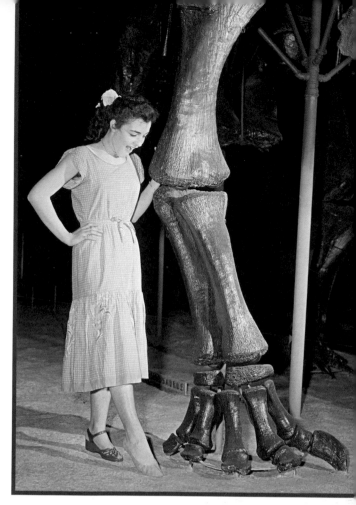

This 1953 visitor to the American Museum of Natural History in New York City compares her foot to the enormous foot of a Stegosaurus *skeleton. The front feet of a* Stegosaurus *each had five toes. Almost like a horse, the tips of these toes were hoof-like. Unlike a horse, however,* Stegosaurus *was rarely able to move very fast!*

school bus. Its back legs were twice as long as its front ones. The back legs were long and straight, while the front legs were turned out to the side. Spongy pads covered the bottoms of its short, wide feet.

Compared to the rest of its body, the animal's head was tiny.

Despite its huge body, Stegosaurus *had a tiny head and brain.*
Some consider it to be among the least intelligent of the dinosaurs.

In fact, its brain was just a little larger than a golf ball. The

dinosaur's mouth ended in a hard beak. The beak helped it tear off

parts of plants to eat. It ground the plants with its stubby teeth.

The dinosaur had a large bundle of nerves near the base of its

tail. The bundle was so big that scientists once thought it was a sec-

ond brain. The tail's sharp spikes were great weapons of protection.

A *Stegosaurus* could **mortally** wound an enemy with one swing of

that mighty tail.

Stegosaurus was hunted by meat-eating predators with amazingly sharp teeth. Fortunately, being hit with Stegosaurus's spiked tail often convinced meat-eating animals to look for their meal somewhere else. Sometimes Stegosaurus successfully scared enemies away by simply swishing its tail from side to side as a warning.

The dinosaur reached a weight of 2 to 3 tons or more. No one

knows what color the animal was or if it had stripes or patterns.

WHAT ABOUT SPIKE'S SPIKE?

Dinosaur bones hold plenty of secrets. They can often tell scientists about how the dinosaur lived and died. By studying the bones of living animals, scientists can also learn a lot. They use that knowledge to look at the bones of long-dead animals.

For example, after a living animal breaks a bone (like the X ray of the human bone at right), scar tissue forms around the break. Scar tissue is denser, or thicker, than normal bone tissue. Sometimes scar tissue forms a little bump over the break. When scientists find bones with unusual dense places or bumps, they believe the animal

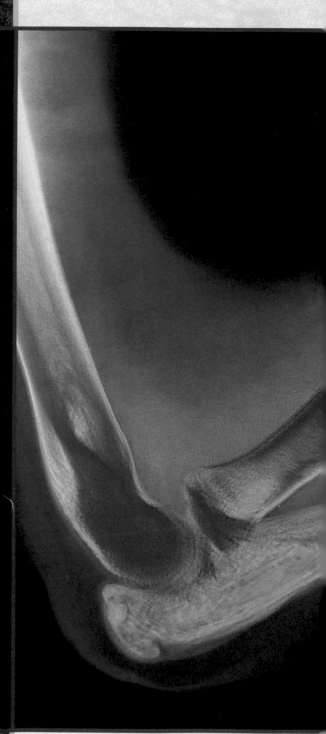

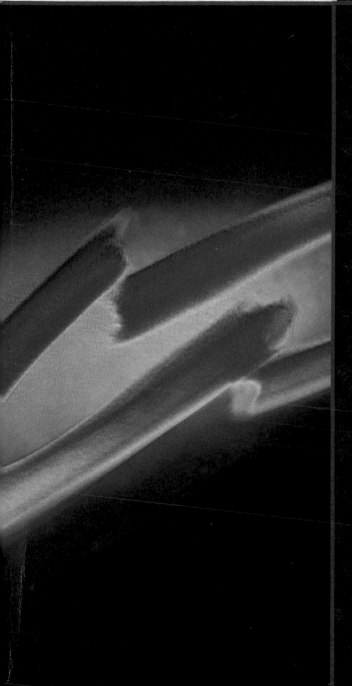

might have had a broken bone that healed. If an animal's bone gets infected, it becomes less dense. In time, it might even be completely eaten away. If the animal cannot fight the infection, it could spread throughout its whole body.

One of Spike's tail spikes looked badly infected when she died. The spike was flatter and shorter than it should have been. With that painful spike, maybe the dinosaur had a hard time defending herself. Maybe she just kept feeling worse and worse all the time. We will never know exactly why Spike died, but her bones tell us some of her story.

Othniel Charles Marsh named several species of dinosaur besides Stegosaurus. *A few of the more famous dinosaurs he named were* Triceratops, Allosaurus, Diplodocus, *and* Apatosaurus.

By looking at the *Stegosaurus* fossils, Marsh first thought that the animal's plates laid down flat on its back. But over the next 10 years, Marsh and his workers made more exciting discoveries. One of the best finds was a *Stegosaurus* skeleton with the bones and plates laid out almost perfectly. Now it was clear that those plates stood up along the dinosaur's back. Still, everyone wondered what they were for.

CHAPTER FOUR

WHY DID IT HAVE
THOSE PLATES?

Some scientists believed that the plates might have been for

protection. But others pointed out that they would not

have been much help. After all, an attacking dinosaur could the

Scientists believe that Stegosaurus *may have been able to move the hard plates on its back to attract a mate or frighten an enemy. Moving special muscles under the skin may have allowed the dinosaur to flap the plates back and forth.*

just bite the *Stegosaurus* in the side. Some scientists today believe that the plates were used for **display.** Maybe the male showed off his plates to attract a female. Maybe the dinosaur stiffened its back and showed those plates to scare off enemies.

Other scientists believe that the plates helped the dinosaur in another way. They have looked closely and found that the plates were not solid. They had tiny tunnels running through them. These tunnels might have been for blood vessels. If the *Stegosaurus* needed to warm up, it could have stood in the sun. The blood running through the plates would have warmed up the animal quickly. If the *Stegosaurus* was too hot, breezes passing by the plates might have cooled the animal down.

If Stegosaurus *used the plates on its back to control body temperature, many scientists believe that the dinosaur may have been cold-blooded. This means that Stegosaurus's body temperature would have been dependent on the outside temperature.*

CHAPTER FIVE

HOW DID A *STEGOSAURUS* SPEND ITS TIME?

To feed its huge body, a *Stegosaurus* probably spent most of its day eating. The *Stegosaurus* was an herbivore (UR-buh-vore). This means that it only ate plants. Its head was low to the ground so it probably could not reach food more than 3 feet (1 m) high. Some

This drawing shows a Stegosaurus *eating low-lying plants. Although many scientists believe that* Stegosaurus *always remained on all fours, some think it may have reared up on its hind legs to reach food higher up. While it might be hard to imagine an animal as large and bulky as* Stegosaurus *doing this, scientists point out that this is how many elephants get their food.*

The plant life in Olympic National Forest in Washington is similar to what Stegosaurus *would have fed upon while it lived. Moss and ferns were soft plants that would have been easy for* Stegosaurus *to eat, given the dinosaur's stubby, weak teeth.*

paleontologists believe that the *Stegosaurus* was able to stand up on its back legs. By doing this, it could reach higher food. But since no one can watch a live *Stegosaurus* as it eats, we may never know.

The *Stegosaurus* did not eat grass because grass had not yet appeared on the earth. Instead, it probably ate ferns and plants called **horsetails,** club mosses, and **conifers.** These grew easily in the warm, humid **environment** of the Jurassic (ju-RASS-ik) period.

CHAPTER SIX

WHAT WAS THE JURASSIC PERIOD?

The Jurassic period was the time span from about 208 million years ago to about 144 million years ago. During that time, Earth was very different from how it is today. Scientists believe that most of Earth's large landmasses (now known as continents) were packed very closely together. During the 64 million years of the Jurassic period, they slowly drifted apart.

Earth was also much warmer than it is now. At the North and South Poles, the air was cool, but not cold. The poles were not even covered with ice. The sea level was higher all over the earth. Many places were lush and green. There was plenty of food for giant, plant-eating dinosaurs.

Dinosaurs dominated Earth then. *Stegosaurus* walked the lands

An artist's idea of what the landscape might have looked like during the Jurassic period. Dinosaurs mysteriously disappeared from Earth during the following period, the Cretaceous (kreh-TAY-shuss) period.

now known as North America, Africa, Europe, and Asia. Other giant

plant-eaters, such as *Diplodocus* (dih-PLOD-uh-kuss) and *Apato-*

saurus (uh-PAT-oh-SORE-uhss), also roamed about. Sharks and

Brachiosaurus *was a giant plant-eater that existed during the Jurassic period. For a while, scientists incorrectly believed that, like* Stegosaurus, Brachiosaurus *had a second brain.*

huge saltwater crocodiles swam the oceans. Flying reptiles and the

first birds circled overhead. Some of the first mammals, tiny mouse-

sized creatures, rustled about on the ground.

The *Stegosaurus* died out around 144 million years ago, just as the Jurassic period was coming to an end. About 77 million years later, the great *Tyrannosaurus rex* appeared. About 65 million years after that, human beings first walked the earth.

Spinosaurus *was one of the dinosaurs that existed during the Cretaceous period. This dinosaur had a series of spines that formed what looked like a fin on its back. Like the plates on* Stegosaurus's *back, these spines may have been used to attract mates, frighten enemies, or help control body temperature.*

OOPS!

Have you ever seen a dinosaur skeleton in a museum? Did you ever wonder how scientists knew which bones went where? When scientists discover a dinosaur skeleton, they take a long look at how the bones are laid out. Sometimes the skeleton is a big mess, with broken bones spread everywhere. But once in a while, a skeleton seems to be laid out nicely. Paleontologists always take lots of notes and pictures when they find a good skeleton because this helps them put it together later. And every time they find a new skeleton, they learn more about the dinosaur.

Stegosaurus plates puzzled everyone for a long time. First, Marsh thought they laid down flat. Later, paleontologists thought they pointed straight up and formed a single row down the dinosaur's back. Museums around the world set up their *Stegosaurus* skeletons to match this idea. Over the years, more skeletons were discovered. Scientists learned more about the creatures with each new find. Now they think the plates were in two rows, with one plate leaning to the left and the next plate leaning to the right. Today, workers at some museums are taking off the plates of their old *Stegosaurus* skeletons. They are rebuilding the skeletons to fit this new idea.

CHAPTER SEVEN

WHAT ELSE CAN WE LEARN?

Everything we know about the *Stegosaurus* and other dinosaurs comes from the fossils they left behind. Sometimes paleontologists find fossils of plant materials where the dinosaur's stomach would have been. This gives them clues to what the dinosaur probably ate. Sometimes imprints from ancient plants are found near the dinosaur. These tell scientists what kinds of plants were in the animal's environ-

In addition to showing how fast a dinosaur moved, footprints can also tell scientists where certain dinosaurs lived and whether they traveled alone or in herds.

These dinosaur skeletons are at the Museum of Natural History in Houston, Texas. Museums sometimes exhibit the original skeletons, but sometimes they show casts, or copies, instead. Dinosaur bones are rare and delicate and are often stored in special museum collections where they are less likely to be damaged.

ment. Sometimes dinosaur footprints give clues as to how fast the animal moved.

Still, there are many questions about *Stegosaurus* that no one has answered. Could it really stand up on its hind legs? How much did it eat every day? How fast could it run? And why did it die out? Paleontologists have puzzled over these questions for years. Maybe someday, you will help solve some of these mysteries.

Glossary

ancient (AYN-shunt) Something that is ancient is very old; from millions of years ago. Fossils are remains of ancient life.

conifers (KON-uh-furz) Conifers are plants that have cones. *Stegosaurus* probably ate conifers.

display (diss-PLAY) A display is a show; or the act of showing off. The plates on *Stegosaurus* may have been used for display.

environment (en-VYE-ruhn-muhnt) An environment is made up of the things that surround a living creature, such as the air and soil. Scientists can sometimes tell what kind of plants were in an ancient animal's environment by studying fossils.

horsetails (HORSS-taylz) Horsetails are ancient sticklike plants. *Stegosaurus* probably ate horsetails.

infection (in-FEK-shuhn) An infection is a disease caused by germs. It was possible for a *Stegosaurus* to develop an infection in one of its spikes.

mortally (MOR-tuhl-lee) Mortally describes an action causing death. *Stegosaurus* could use its spiky tail to mortally wound an enemy.

reptile (REP-tile) A reptile is an air-breathing animal with a backbone and is usually covered with scales or plates. *Stegosaurus* was a reptile.

Did You Know?

▶ *Stegosaurus* is the state fossil of Colorado.

▶ It took a U.S. Army helicopter to carry Spike's skeleton to a place where scientists could work on it.

▶ Some Stegosaurs had large spines sticking out from their shoulders.

▶ A *Stegosaurus* skeleton discovered by M. P. Felch is now on display in a museum where people have nicknamed it 'The Roadkill.'

The Geologic Time Scale

TRIASSIC PERIOD

Date: 248 million to 208 million years ago

Fossils: *Coelophysis, Cynodont, Desmatosuchus, Eoraptor, Gerrothorax, Peteinosaurus, Placerias, Plateosaurus, Postosuchus, Procompsognathus, Riojasaurus, Saltopus, Teratosaurus, Thecodontosaurus*

Distinguishing Features: For the most part, the climate in the Triassic period was hot and dry. The first true mammals appeared during this period, as well as turtles, frogs, salamanders, and lizards. Corals could also be found in oceans at this time, although large reefs such as the ones we have today did not yet exist. Evergreen trees made up much of the plant life.

JURASSIC PERIOD

Date: 208 million to 144 million years ago

Fossils: *Allosaurus, Anchisaurus, Apatosaurus, Barosaurus, Brachiosaurus, Ceratosaurus, Compsognathus, Cryptoclidus, Dilophosaurus, Diplodocus, Eustreptospondylus, Hybodus, Janenschia, Kentrosaurus, Liopleurodon, Megalosaurus, Opthalmosaurus, Rhamphorhynchus, Saurolophus, Segisaurus, Seismosaurus, Stegosaurus, Supersaurus, Syntarsus, Ultrasaurus, Vulcanodon, Xiaosaurus*

Distinguishing Features: The climate of the Jurassic period was warm and moist. The first birds appeared during this period. Plant life was also greener and more widespread. Sharks began swimming in Earth's oceans. Although dinosaurs didn't even exist at the beginning of the Triassic period, they ruled Earth by Jurassic times. There was a minor mass extinction toward the end of the Jurassic period.

CRETACEOUS PERIOD

Date: 144 million to 65 million years ago

Fossils: *Acrocanthosaurus, Alamosaurus, Albertosaurus, Anatotitan, Ankylosaurus, Argentinosaurus, Bagaceratops, Baryonyx, Carcharodontosaurus, Carnotaurus, Centrosaurus, Chasmosaurus, Corythosaurus, Didelphodon, Edmontonia, Edmontosaurus, Gallimimus, Gigantosaurus, Hadrosaurus, Hypsilophodon, Iguanodon, Kronosaurus, Lambeosaurus, Leaellynasaura, Maiasaura, Megaraptor, Muttaburrasaurus, Nodosaurus, Ornithocheirus, Oviraptor, Pachycephalosaurus, Panoplosaurus, Parasaurolophus, Pentaceratops, Polacanthus, Protoceratops, Psittacosaurus, Quaesitosaurus, Saltasaurus, Sarcosuchus, Saurolophus, Sauropelta, Saurornithoides, Segnosaurus, Spinosaurus, Stegoceras, Stygimoloch, Styracosaurus, Tapejara, Tarbosaurus, Therizinosaurus, Thescelosaurus, Torosaurus, Trachodon, Triceratops, Troodon, Tyrannosaurus rex, Utahraptor, Velociraptor*

Distinguishing Features: The climate of the Cretaceous period was fairly mild. Flowering plants first appeared in this period, and many modern plants developed. With flowering plants came a greater diversity of insect life. Birds further developed into two types: flying and flightless. A wider variety of mammals also existed. At the end of this period came a great mass extinction that wiped out the dinosaurs, along with several other groups of animals.

How to Learn More

At the Library

Lambert, David, Darren Naish, and Liz Wyse. *Dinosaur Encyclopedia.*
New York: DK Publishing, 2001.

Landau, Elaine. *Stegosaurus.* Danbury, Conn.: Children's Press, 1999.

On the Web

Visit our home page for lots of links about *Stegosaurus:*
http://www.childsworld.com/links.html
Note to Parents, Teachers, and Librarians: We routinely verify our
Web links to make sure they're safe, active sites—so encourage
your readers to check them out!

Places to Visit or Contact

AMERICAN MUSEUM OF NATURAL HISTORY
*To view numerous dinosaur fossils, as well as
the fossils of several ancient mammals*
Central Park West at 79th Street
New York, NY 10024-5192
212/769-5100

CARNEGIE MUSEUM OF NATURAL HISTORY
*To view a variety of dinosaur skeletons, as well as fossils related
to other reptiles, amphibians, and fish that are now extinct*
4400 Forbes Avenue
Pittsburgh, PA 15213
412/622-3131

DINOSAUR DEPOT
To see the dinosaur named Spike
330 Royal Gorge Blvd.
Cañon City, CO 81212
800/987-6379

DINOSAUR NATIONAL MONUMENT
To view a huge deposit of dinosaur bones in a natural setting
4545 East Highway 40
Dinosaur, CO 81610-9724
or
DINOSAUR NATIONAL MONUMENT (QUARRY)
11625 East 1500 South
Jensen, UT 84035
435/781-7700

MUSEUM OF THE ROCKIES
To see real dinosaur fossils, as well as robotic replicas
Montana State University
600 West Kagy Boulevard
Bozeman, MT 59717-2730
406/994-2251 or 406/994-DINO (3466)

NATIONAL MUSEUM OF NATURAL HISTORY
(SMITHSONIAN INSTITUTION)
To see several dinosaur exhibits and take special behind-the-scenes tours
10th Street and Constitution Avenue, N.W.
Washington, DC 20560-0166
202/357-2700

Index

About the Author

Susan H. Gray has bachelor's and master's degrees in zoology, and has taught college-level courses in biology. She first fell in love with fossil hunting while studying paleontology in college. In her 25 years as an author, she has written many articles for scientists and researchers, and many science books for children. Susan enjoys gardening, traveling, and playing the piano. She and her husband, Michael, live in Cabot, Arkansas.